caught./

caught./

ISBN 9780692227657

from the past: lining

sca
led across
ca   pture
s ca;rred l   asted
seari   n g   fl
ash/
list l ess

beauty   steal

till   edtempt
nas   ti   ly;chang
e.   bea   ring

withinsideyoulining

beautylove

static, apparent striving vintage patience,
belies the devil starting of
my wholeness complete audacity
believe a scant inducing
inoculation dismal dying hear,
perceive benign and dire
candor, ardor of betwixt, betwixt
of desire. déchirer en deux
et finis tout de ma monde.
static, apparent striving for liberated
discipline. dive atop into myself
le vérité de mon vie, the
bewildered mouse becomes an
intricate part of my heart,
soul.. believe my trials.
déchirer en deux mon coeur.
static apparent strive for
discipline style of mire, dire
accented insert, benign the
devil lies, the devious occur to
the part of fois de mon
Vérité, audacity complete and
dying imminent. survive. kill.
remain, et finis mon destruction.

You still when these to naught has sunk and all
Abhorred abundantly, the subtleties
Have ushered back from where it lie from fall,
The previous decline. Immortal ties.
Though tried and lost these fears have yet to kill.
All love and fame to nothingness now seem
A brittle hope, false motivation still;
Though cloudy symbols huge have yet to deem
This heart worthy to even trace their fierce
And wanton ways, shadows of passion. Tears
Have criticized the sheltered thoughts and guile,
Uprooting these, a cavalcade of fears,
To steer away from hope itself; wanted
Unrelenting love replaced with doubt instead.

seared
an obvious recollection
myriads dire
pains
visions dreams
utopian_known
hate for   chance
change
a past recollection
clear
pursuit dance

escape
not allowed
green
why
scenes
stillness
progression
deny,   refine,   deny
reiteration
too fucked
c'est la vie :

though fearful of the casual eyes and harsh
judgemental attitudes, alive more now
than oft before my soul breathes deep. just as
untimely circumstance presents truly
a troubled thing, i keep in faith that time
will bring the resolute confirmation.
noble ways are all that remain, between
many sharp words and stolen glances. a
hope so great creates tension, at least that
i can confirm. weathering the trials
will likely be the most difficult of
things i ever attempted, but when i
am eagerly pursuing it all, the
beauty calls and will be coy no longer.

familiar. /

shuttered; battered. lost.
casual(ly) embraced, yet braced unhinged
through reckless/glances
full romance and trouble mirrored past

unknown, however familiar.
bad choices. lies. unfair
same choices.. again. : ____

waiting, hoping dropped
and-all the flood returns

cast_aside. and/and and.   and.,,...

gone;;

kindle

spark.   battle.   freeze.

finally a   gain.
the restless_ness now   ceased
thoroughly overwhelmed
  , but moving through   and forward./

slowly. calm. enchanted.
  trouble/scrap e.

kindle.   caught;   dream.

had not she first gazed deep, azure brimming
laughter, contentment so sublime, into
these curiously naive eyes, maybe
the last of many years would have been void,
as those of the all-too-bleak past. of late,
those eyes – those gorgeous flames – engulfed every
waking moment as it did of the vast
eternity of slumbers' reveries:
intensifyingly haunting in a
perfect mode. stale air cramped the room, became
thick, leaden as she passed. breathing, walking,
all thngs simple complex in the presence
of fair royalty, perfection rich. time
accumulated, grace deepened. growing.
still the fixed gaze on that glorious day
lingered. latent content in that blank stare
of angels eyes had soon to tear into
surreal, reality then thereafter,
ever so gently pushing forth. array
of noble things – choses de mal – within
such brief a confine of time, had passed in
supreme eloquence from those fair cold spheres
direct to an inadequate equipped soul.

had not i been subdued complete,
            entrusted insecurities
that none should comprehend. when i,
            naïve and young, lulled quick
to sleep, and, half-asleep, aroused
            to dream of love, lust, and hate.
every word preceded a kiss,
            then more, till love and fame indeed
depressed to naught, leaving my
            shattered heart wrought only by the
gift she had given. then on this
            beautiful day, when all her words
of love and sweetness were muffled
            finally, while, fast-asleep, she
was roused to death. my doll, little
            angel's deep blue eyes now were as

They should, perfect in their stillness.
yo   u should   not have
as sumingit   all
grows on you
tie   dd   own

lost
dri   ven
l   ost

cau ghtup   torn
tor   mented
you i
de c   id e
f   or

lovehate

when I speak
into   your in.nocent eyes
___lay honest

words cannot contend
the / depth
of your brilliant flames

conversing

even things;
that add seem
whilst add unto
multiplying woes
to divide
the reciprocal of
the infinite

undeniably consuming contain,
among other mild things, les choses de
rein, within their sight glorious the
myriads of silencing reactions,
the masses of unretainable blinds,
distractions. i merely seek to
help. missing the audacity of being
one, having the whole of your attention
centered, and became spoiled that it was
quite an overwhelming shock when longer
not was i the prey; to glances had been
diminished to a smaller number though
still greatly in effect and the sighs that
no angelic host could imitate to
house what it may were even more confined.

in heat, the waves washing all our troubles
ashore. swept out with the current. happenings
cast aside, alight, afoot __ altered patience through
wandering blue skies. rain. clouds. whispering
melting hearts and hard eyes.

all that falls.

in cold, silence threatened by the rain. inspired
yet disabled. trapped in the metal bridge forged
pushed into, away, toward __ figured distance in
infinite subtlety would ease the pain. screaming
cautious minds and lesser thoughts.

all that falls. /

separating
prediction
caught up
description
holding

/ envisions the likeliness
absolute profoundness of
lapsed inconceivabilities and
further irritations therefore.

inhale
lonely passions
false can't does
chance. charge.
just live
down fallen perfection

exhale
residue confusion
naïve shouldn't, does
change chance.
truly live
continue; falling perfection

tears
dreams
outweigh
fiction
falsely
pushed
aside
living
loving
past
cried
all
out

under th(rough for)th away
signed. forever, but not - yet

never - - maybe / but better
trash and.and precocious still

stale stripped bad and
great stal;led bitter wait

/

inevitable
envied the likeness darkness – desirous
indubitably so far sovereign. free
/ contiguous. And these pious
apparitions between, a stately
principle for

the
black
and
white
succession

i couldn't think this'd be
  such a
trouble, doubling force force
  in course predicted
                prescripted
 from (the previous time

peering inside, took all
brought out the pain, it chilling call
i'm falling again. hearing:calling
  longing for something i'd never
solve
   never, though in fall^ this way
   i severed dreams to see

heard you in the whisper
          of your longing eyes
everything you say is taken for
granted
spark_ing seeming diamond
   through heavens guise
   subtle surp)rised
     i can't know where

  i see you waiting for an answer
i'm hurting myself for a while
   i   never tried to die again

Through and amidst the thinning confusion
It remains blazing, never ceasing; the
Rising circumstances and numerous
Opportunities, which are half my days;
Their unusual and consequential
Results unknown force my disturbing thoughts
And, though unrecognized, my behavior,
Which lie in itself foreign to all I
Thought of my purpose and reasons for being.
Cast down thoughts of woe and weariness of
Unreproached for through you lie the only
Gate to which brought me through into this state
Of intense and complete weltering and
Which I accredit seemly eternal.
Azure, compelling and hazy, distraught
By that which ever-enduring refuse
To die or lessen slightly, abstract in
Mind, yet tangibly felt, and hitherto
Intensely overwhelming. Reprieve and
Condolence accounted therefore to aid
Reconstruction; the hurt and joy birthed through
Bittersweet interviews amongst which can
Contend with behavior of various
Thought up by the great minds. Between all seemed
Disarrayed in both high opposition
Substantial and unity embodied
Within aversion, but no mysteries
Solved yet joyful I abide and content
Remain until bliss, bliss soon impending

Lay before me and whose grasp for so long
Hardly fathomed or have capacity to
Even understand; lay before me in
Wait, mine to hold an cherish, if only
Action is implemented, forcefully
Not, but subtle and transparent, serene
In all its ways.

// separating
predic-
tion
caught up
description
holding

defeat the
purpose.

control the
passive . sublime .

charitable.
wired cold and dark.
frail. empty

just a wish…

undone .

alas – confusion and deception born
in light of recent success – but young blood
not of – running thick within a forlorn,
surly demeanor. superfluous flood
minds eye and imminently perception
nulled, like ancient omen justly divined
and foretold. perchance would there a vision,
slight sliver of faint hope ablaze, confined
though eminent in ambiguity
be unveiled, then would reveries far from
my reality resurrected be.
submerged incantations betwixt lost sum
up to remain, confined though revived it
lives, throughout should not continue counterfeit.

the tendrils of black
red matte circumference   the
shiny eyes of pools ,
indecent very pools

tendril of black
red matte
seeped to bleak
predatory eyes

visage of the bleak
with lies
predatory eyes,   the
catlike stationary

lions vision and
a visage purely
timid.

stepped
engaged

violated / throughout

al.to.gether
silent

\

envied the thoughts of continued violence, i can't continue
involved entwined other a fact of indubitable contiguous.
invariably zygote maze of mirrored hurts shattered over
the stagnant reverie chemist of all colors, thoughts of all
woes wallowed through the endless vastness. bleakness
reigned over the environment struggled with the mindset.
and still i move from past tribulations. benign words
and meaningless meanings. false things and facades of
great enchantment seem to blind, hazy the truth. behind
words. love entowered the violence, hate induced the
mind. blood smeared the sky and smote the masses. trials
seem to fade while shimmering dims and things of choses
hideux est tres… thought once of dreams which come
of trials tribulatory paradise seems so far and waiting
seems so hard. adrenaline veils and curtains deep within:
ambiguities of cast down lies and serpents of various sizes.
fire blazing and molten flesh. screaming goes on and life
passes by. still hurt and pain still subsides. too tremendous.
eloquence has shattered faded into existence. the effusion
of things go like the shore in its intrinsic and unpredictable
behavior; though of predictability there will be never,
naught seems to hinder the familiarity of witchcraft. fears
of the moon that invulnerables satellite. foe is to come and
fire is to weigh down upon the incessant.

c'est

    heavy
isthe hardest

          part   without

  thedream   that is
it went.   and changed.

fraught within starry nights and scattered are
numerous perils haunting every move
suggested, through action not granted. marred
not of things tangible, in which to prove
takes none, but surreal, existing only
within the confines of the mind. simple
inducing contempt to be free
in the natural, but liking loves will
question. even obvious. the war in
full disposition lay beneath and truth –
basis of life, which is love – begins
losing fervor and vivacity; both
real, still hidden by façade. my ardor
grows with each day, but that cannot stop the war.

shall i happily decline
these; unattained values,
visions really of thoughtless
benumbed entices – black
and white of colorful hues.

Will many tomorrows

Never be achieved or will
hints of diligence – e'en
if it is naught to become;
with that sense in the least,

Be e'er so subtlely declined

thoughts of these shant be,
                controlling

fire throughout
set upon...   continuing ...   endowed

mischief of

. . besides
this   cannot   that
will   imagine .
against my

wi   sh   es   to
transpire
a   gain   st .
op   it   al

ready ; yet ..
it does   occur.
still . .

holding on, dreaming fiercely
romantic
won't try
figuring
estimating
difficult, too different
please
let it go… definitely
fighting
chance doesn't stop
stop
you are not you
be
you just you
don't
want such obviousness
tragedy
just like me
dreamer
reminiscent of times
romantic
cannot be denied
stubborn
i'm so sorry, dear.

past woes hadn't believe
undoubt beside unvaried
erase false classification
got when stuck believe unveil
crying doesn't continue last
beside can't counterfeit
continue felt believe all
unfound whence undying
want finds alas consuming
believe uncan't deep stake continue.

the best
so. . i thought afire

consumed all
but. . try harder

withal
incensed and blessed

indifferences
worried

rain. . of tried sums fire
divinely vile

unexpressed
withal gratitude
allowance
dealt those: fatefully
wandering
unspoken – convergence
of desires
from remains, forth
enticing

Consume these matters
Facades, double-meanings,
Misinterpretations true,
Pain of things unseen – overwrought
And underestimated throughout.
Resume all, continue toil stricken
Ever-enduring provisions, fair
Intrigue of truth, blazon fires
For purity, open lines
Communicating still.
Sovereign ardor most.

couldnt let
the best of myself
look through - fall through
captured
feature undo
simple. complex. curious
none, but all
free through mired hope
sorry
truly

she came calling one early morning
she showed her swoon of thorns
she whispered softly to tell
how she had been wronged

close___eyes
imagine all night
could not hide tears
wished away

angers violent still l___ silent, . at home
this decadence seared in
millions remember you alone

close your eyes
imagine everything
don't hide your tears
sent to wash away those years...
maybe one can

chased many oceans lay
between life are many
portions hope found meaning
closed eyes
imagined
with hidden tears
washed away

I unbutton
Bring unrelenting
... self-centered trough
whilst filthy stance subvert
frame – nerve

II descry
... lipread perquisites
enjoy
must (er   protest (ant

III tie
_ counter-productive
impiety expand ...
_quizzical burial
pacify

For untold and unseen wrought with / forlorn
Hues compose in incandescent soul, cast
Upon unveiling lies, those horrid things
From naught but my own flesh torn by the last
And first of offenses committed / of
Unparalleled fervor. Overshadow
Not fain / glances but restlessness above
Trepidation; vivacity's borough
Delved deep amongst mysterious / of love
Of hate, obsession, infatuation
Released in thorough intervals betwixt
Agonizing self-transcription
Betokened solely in those spheres with
Flames of ardor, where pools of beauty writhe.

Ihateyouveneverseenwill
diewithwordsweveneverespoke
w
i
t
h
everyssuchindecent
o
u
t
love
m
e

Collide without flying has
become a vagabond of all
triumphs. where forth
the mire pays too little and
beauty overwhelmed. These
collisions often believe in
themselves to be much
more than in others'
reality. Must infusions
of bitterness seek to dwell
amongst the greatest of joy?
no, it's the most
miniscule of joys that
are interwoven into that
tangled web of hurt.
why, therefore, can the
trials resulted by these
indifferent collisions Lose,
at least, the sting that
so overwrought sense
and interpretation falsely?

missing
monster________

Blue skies_travelled
unknown
fearless.ly

matched. thought. clarity
prevailed
falsely

undone_preposterous_in
love
callous
metal heart/believe
caution –
passion.

benign words condensed by overlapping
silent pain emotions defy trapping
true and noble character persisting
even within trials that cannot rely
on physical lies and shadows darkness
has seen not in time or between all that
sonically is surreal, blankly repress
temper, behavior, and traits being rich
in its forlorn intrinsic intellect
and sesquipedalian in every
work or move had little to no effect
where simplistic caught in reality
would serve better than words of wayward and
incomprehensibility ever can.

no more through
the flames
of red blackish
____matte will

prey to predator
control little
eyes of grey
____lions weight ,

yet pretty .
left behind the distance ,
chalking white

am ong the
j ackals,, t he wolves of

those that hunt in gen eral
forfeiting most. . al most
al lof those th ngs

foreign false , ye t fast an
d past wispers different
mysteries s eem t o

hold ac countable.
piercing those fierce
magical sphe res for with
out

meanness
facad es fade

catch my
me lody

between . i should have
known

before

ididn't . i wouldn't near

cannot

we didn't . fresh kill

however long
fight
forever how

until drab, broken
tilled
everything unearthed

until rain
snow
sun and all has gone

distant - unbroken
fought

www.ingramcontent.com/pod-product-compliance
Lightning Source LLC
Chambersburg PA
CBHW061344040426
42444CB00011B/3071
* 9 7 8 0 6 9 2 2 2 7 6 5 7 *